THE
FINAL MYSTERY

. . . PEOPLE ARE BORN AND PEOPLE DIE.

THE FINAL MYSTERY

STANLEY KLEIN

DOUBLEDAY & COMPANY, INC.

GARDEN CITY, NEW YORK

1974

ISBN: 0-385-09133-8 Trade
0-385-06184-6 Prebound
Library of Congress Catalog Card Number 70–180084

DEDICATED TO THE THREE GIRLS IN MY LIFE . . .
Lei, Nan, and Jamie
And with special thanks to Tom Aylesworth
for his infinite patience and to Alice Schick for
her talented assistance . . .

CONTENTS

THE
FINAL MYSTERY

CHAPTER ONE
WHAT IS DEATH?

EVERYTHING HAS A BEGINNING AND AN END. Life, too, begins and ends. Birth and death are parts of life. Without one we could not have the other.

Almost everywhere in the world birth is a time of happiness. It is the beginning of a new life. And life is something we all know about. We know how it feels to move our hands and kick our feet. We know how good it feels to eat something we like or laugh at something funny.

We know life has its good times and its bad times, but the most important thing is that we *know* what it means to be alive. And we rarely fear something we know about.

But what do we know about death? We know that animals which once breathed and moved about in life no longer breathe or move in death. We know that plants which once grew and blossomed no longer grow and develop flowers. We know that when a member of our family, a friend, or a pet dies, we feel sad. We know that death means that a life has ended. But we know little more. Is life like an endless, dreamless sleep? Does something of a person remain alive after his body dies?

These are questions that the living cannot answer. We might have our own ideas about what death is like but we really do not know. The ideas we do have often come from our culture or religion. But each culture and religion has different ideas too. So the true meaning of death remains a mystery.

Most often a mystery offers excitement, a challenge, and to most people, a little fear. People tend to fear something they don't know about or don't know what to expect from it. So in many societies, death is something people grow up fearing. And in their fear they do silly and strange things. Some families won't discuss death. They believe that talking about it might make it happen. When a relative is near death, parents sometimes hide the fact from their children or refuse to talk about it. When a death does occur in a family, some people begin to feel guilt. They think of all the things they should have done for that person before he died. Sometimes very small children feel angry when a family member dies because they think the person left them because they didn't love them. Other children begin to fear that they too will soon die. Of course, most children have long lives ahead of them and have no reason to become afraid.

But these strange thoughts often do go through a person's mind when death occurs. They are strange thoughts, but they are normal thoughts. Feeling sad for a person or pet you loved is normal. But death is normal too, and if we could learn more about it perhaps we would fear it less.

Because so much about death remains a mystery, people have long been fascinated with the subject. Courses about death are now being taught at colleges and universities. Magazines are filling pages with articles exploring the meaning of death. One of the magazines devotes all of its pages to the subject. And scientists continue to gather evidence to understand it better.

One researcher, Dr. Russell Noyes, Jr., of the University of Iowa, is studying the thoughts of people before they die. He recently translated a report written in 1892 by a Swiss geologist and mountain climber. The geologist, Albert Heim, wrote about interviews he had with thirty people who survived falls from the jagged walls of the Alps. Each of these people described in detail how they felt as they were falling to what they believed was their death. Dr. Noyes also reported his findings about peoples' feelings as they survived more recent, near fatal accidents.

He found that the experience of almost dying included three stages of thought. The first stage was one of fear and fighting to save oneself. The person struggled against death. When there seemed to be no further chance of survival, the person's fear disappeared and he almost began to welcome death. Then the second emotion began to take place. People began to recall the happy memories of the past. They saw their lives "flash" before them. Dr. Noyes believes that this "life review" was the person's defense against the thought of death. Finally, the person seemed to be overcome with a complete feeling of peace.

Does the study of Dr. Noyes truly describe the feelings of someone who believes he is about to die? Are these the last feelings of life? Do all people share the same emotions at this time? We really don't know. Every question man seems to answer about death just raises more questions. But as long as there are unanswered questions, the search will go on.

Although we may not know what death is, or even what to expect, it has always been important to know when death occurred. Until recently, it was believed that a person died when his heart stopped beating. Without a pumping heart, blood cannot flow throughout the body, cells cannot be nourished, organs cannot function, and breathing cannot take place. Death was confirmed when a body no longer reacted to normal life function and all reflexes had stopped.

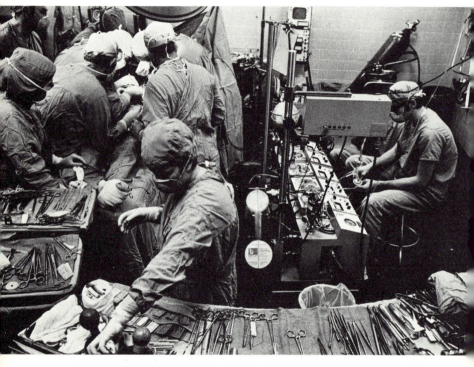

OPEN-HEART SURGERY, ONCE THOUGHT IMPOSSIBLE, IS PERFORMED DAILY THROUGHOUT THE WORLD. AS HIGHLY TRAINED SURGEONS OPEN AND REPAIR A DAMAGED HEART, MACHINES CONTINUE TO CLEAN THE BLOOD AND PUMP IT THROUGH THE PATIENT'S BODY.

There seemed to be no reason to go beyond this simple test to determine death. But in the past few years, modern medicine has made even the one sure thing about death unsure. Doctors now know that a person with a stilled heart is not necessarily dead. For if a stilled heart means death, there are many people walking around today who have been dead. Sometimes after a serious accident or operation, a patient's heart suddenly stops beating. Doctors have found that if they act quickly, the patient may be saved from death. Doctors can start the heart beating again by a chemical stimulant, electric shock, or by massaging the heart by hand.

During some types of major surgery, especially open-heart surgery, the surgeons cannot work if the patient's heart is steadily moving and pumping blood. They can connect the patient's blood circulation system to a machine outside the body. This machine does the work of the heart during the operation and the doctors can work on the stilled heart. Later the repaired heart is reconnected and can start beating normally again.

Were the people whose hearts stopped and

then started again dead at one time and brought back to life? Or was the old definition of death "dead wrong?" For years doctors puzzled over this question. Then in 1967, people all over the world began asking it. For on December 3 of that year a surgeon, Dr. Christiaan Barnard of Cape Town, South Africa, performed the world's first heart transplant on a human being.

Dr. Barnard had assembled a highly trained team of doctors and nurses to do organ transplants. The team had done a successful kidney transplant. Dr. Barnard had done experimental heart transplants on dogs. He now felt that he and his team were ready to try a human heart transplant.

Dr. Barnard knew the risks. He knew that if a human transplant was to be done, it must be done on a patient who would likely die of heart disease within a few days. He also knew that the human body tends to reject anything that is not part of itself. Therefore one body normally rejects an organ from another body. Dr. Barnard would have to have a heart from a donor who had blood and tissue as similar to those of his patient as possible. He would also have to give drugs to help the patient's body accept the new heart.

Dr. Barnard had a difficult time trying to convince his colleagues about the wisdom of his plan. Many felt that a human transplant was not possible at the time. They believed he had little chance of success, for like Dr. Barnard, they knew the unsolved problems of rejection. But Dr. Barnard finally convinced the hospital authorities to agree to his plan.

Finding a patient was easy. Mr. Louis Washkansky was a desperately ill patient. He was very weak from a diseased heart and doctors believed that he was about to die. There seemed little hope. Mr. Washkansky agreed to be Dr. Barnard's patient.

Finding a donor was much harder. The doctors agreed that the donor had to be pronounced dead before the heart could be removed. Yet if too much time was wasted, the heart could no longer be used. Time went by. Mr. Washkansky waited and grew weaker. Dr. Barnard and his team waited too, and wondered if a donor would ever be found. Everything was ready, but there was no donor. Then, after three long weeks, Dr. Barnard received word that a young woman had been struck by a car, had a brain injury, and was dying.

The operating room was prepared. The woman was brought to the hospital. Her brain activity had stopped. The neurosurgeon, a doctor whose specialty is the brain, considered the woman dead. Still, a machine was keeping her breathing and the heart still beating.

Dr. Barnard made tests and determined that the woman's blood and tissue were a good match with Washkansky's. Her heart was in good condition.

Mr. Washkansky was made ready to receive the new heart. Then the wait began all over again. For when the machine which kept the donor's heart beating was shut off, the heart kept beating. Barnard refused to remove the heart until it stopped beating by itself. For fifteen agonizing minutes the heart beat on. With every new beat, Dr. Barnard knew his chances and those of Mr. Washkansky grew less and less. Time was critical. Finally the donor's heart stopped. In minutes, her chest cavity was opened, then painstakingly, with every skill developed by the highly trained team, her heart was removed. It was rushed to an adjoining operating room where Washkansky lay, and transplanted into his body.

But would the new heart work? It had not received oxygen or blood for fifteen minutes. All during the operation, Mr. Washkansky's circulatory system had been connected to a machine. If the machine was disconnected now, would the new heart beat by itself? Twice the doctors stopped the pump. Twice the new heart failed. They tried again. This time the heart kept beating. The operation was a success. Dr. Barnard and Louis Washkansky had made history.

For about eighteen months after that first heart transplant, several doctors performed many heart transplant operations. The record of patient survival was not good. Some died during the operation. Others died within a few weeks of diseases they could not combat because of anti-rejection drugs for their new hearts. Louis Washkansky lived only eighteen days after his transplant. He died of double pneumonia. But his new heart had worked.

Only a few of the heart transplant patients lived more than a few months. In spite of large doses of anti-rejection drugs that sometimes had unpleasant side effects, most patients rejected their new hearts. Today, very few heart transplants are performed. Most doctors want to wait until they learn more about rejection.

Even though heart transplant operations are no longer common, they raised important questions about the definition of death. Most doctors agree that a person can be dead even though his heart is still beating. They define death as an irreversible coma. That is, they say that if a person is unconscious, does not move, either voluntarily or involuntarily, does not respond to anything, shows no brain activity on an electroencephalagram machine, and cannot breathe without mechanical aid, that person is dead.

Still, the old definition of death seems to linger on. Dr. Barnard refused to remove a heart from a donor until the heart was still. One American doctor found himself in legal trouble because he removed a heart from a patient in an irreversible coma when the heart still beat.

More and more people are beginning to agree that death means irreversible coma. But the law has not yet caught up with this new

OFTEN PEOPLE THINK OF THEIR PETS AS MEMBERS OF THE FAMILY. WHEN A PET DIES SOME PEOPLE EVEN BURY IT IN A SPECIAL PET CEMETERY OR IN A CEMETERY NEAR RELATIVES OF THE FAMILY.

thinking. Legal experts continue to examine existing laws about death. It may take many years before there is complete agreement about its definition. Until that time, the mystery surrounding death remains—not only what it is, but when it happens. And as long as these questions remain, people will continue to believe what they wish. But you must remember that most people fear death not because of what is known but, rather, what is unknown.

CHAPTER TWO
THE BELIEFS
OF ANCIENT PEOPLE

ALL GOVERNMENTS, IN EVERY COUNTRY, MAKE laws about death. The laws tell doctors and families what they must do when a person dies. The laws state how to prepare for burial and where to bury the dead. The law says what records must be made and what will happen to the dead person's belongings or property.

For as long as there have been people on earth, death has demanded special ways of behaving from the survivors. Archaeologists, sci-

.entists who study the ways of ancient peoples, have found graves that give clues to how early man thought of death. Many thousands of years ago, early men, who used stone tools and wore animal skins, believed death was a special event, an important part of human life.

All persons have some of the same needs and problems. Everyone needs food to eat; a safe place to live, and clothes to wear. Almost every person needs to belong to a group, or social system; to be protected by some form of government; and to have ways of handling important events such as birth and death. But each group finds its own ways of meeting these needs and solving these problems. From the very beginning of man's history, people have tried to understand and explain the mystery of death. So it isn't surprising that separate groups of people living in different parts of the world, at different times, have differed from each other in their ideas and customs, or ways of behaving, about death. What is puzzling is that some groups who never knew each other, who looked, acted, and believed differently about many things, had very much the same ideas and customs dealing with death.

More than five thousand years ago, people lived along the shores of the islands that are now called Japan. Although these people did not live in caves, they looked and acted very much like our idea of cavemen. They hadn't discovered metals. They used roughly made stone tools. They were just beginning to learn how to make pottery. They were just beginning to learn how to farm. Luckily, they had the sea to provide most of their food. Shellfish, found at the water's edge, was boiled so that the shells were easier to open.

After they were finished eating they tossed their heaps of empty shells on the ground. Along with the empty shells went the stubborn clams whose shells refused to open. It probably didn't take too many shellfish dinners before the small heap grew into a big one—a great big mound. Probably, when it did, the people moved to a place where they could start another mound. And these mounds of discarded shells are important because they tell us about these ancient people. They were used as graves, and thousands of years later skeletons were found buried in the shell mounds.

When the first shell-mound graves were

discovered, some people thought that the ancient islanders had had no respect for their dead. It seemed that they just discarded them along with the empty shells. But later searchers found that some of the skeleton bones had been painted red. We don't know what meaning was attached to the red color, but it does show that these people treated death as a special event. Burial in the shell mounds was a ceremony, not an insult. The shell mounds had to be second burial places because time had to go by before the bones could be painted.

Scientists also found that the bones were in good condition after thousands of years, largely because they lay inside the shell mounds. The chemical composition of the clean water-washed shells helped to preserve the bones. Although these ancients had no knowledge of chemistry, they may have known that the bones would last a long time among the shells and placed them there because they wanted to save them. Most of the skeletons inside the shell mounds were lying curled up, with the legs bent and the knees at the chest. Some investigators have guessed that they were arranged to imitate the way an unborn child lives inside its mother's body. If this is the reason, it means that these primitive people understood the naturalness of death. That they saw life as a circle, and a person returning to the earth in the same way he came.

In those early times, the younger, the smaller, the weaker a person was, the less chance he or she had of staying alive. Many children probably died of small problems such as a toothache or a splinter, just because man hadn't learned what to do about them. Searchers of the shell heaps, every so often find bones, especially children's bones, stored in clay jars. Sometimes, too, a small skeleton buried under the shells had a stone resting on its head or chest, or was lying in the center of a circle of stones.

The people of the shell mounds left no written records, so we can never be sure of the real meanings of these strange burials. But some people have guessed that special care was taken to make sure that the dead would not return to harm the living. Possibly, the ancient people believed that a person who died before he was old might come back to hurt his relatives for allowing him to die. A stone placed on his body might hold him down. He might not be able to escape easily from a clay jar or a stone circle.

We can never be sure exactly what meaning death had to these ancient people of Japan. But we can be certain that it was an important part of their lives.

Long after the shell-heap builders of Japan had disappeared, another group of people called the Scythians lived on the grasslands of what is now Russia. The Scythians left no written records either, but we know a great deal about their customs because of a number of tombs that have been discovered. Some of these tombs are twenty-five hundred years old.

The Scythians were horsemen and warriors. They were ruled by chiefs who had great power over their people. The chiefs were the most important people in life, and the most important people in death, as well.

We know that the Scythians believed in a life after death. After a person died, he would wake up in the afterlife and continue very much as he had on earth. So, a poor soldier would be a poor soldier in the afterlife, while a chief would be a chief. It was important for the living to prepare the dead for their afterlives, and, of course, the amount of preparation depended on the dead person's position in life. Probably, the simpler burials of the less important people have disappeared. Up to the present, all the burial tombs that have been discovered are those of chiefs or other important men.

Although they believed in an afterlife, the Scythians thought of death as a time of sorrow. The dead person would continue to exist, but he would never again have contact with the living. The living would miss him. Maybe the great ceremonies that surrounded the death of chiefs were meant to help the living accept sadness more easily while preparing the dead for their new world.

The plains horsemen did not have the funeral as soon as someone died. Instead, they set aside two times a year for funerals. One burial time came in the spring; the other in the fall. Therefore, when someone died, it was necessary to keep the body until burial time. The Scythians did not know the methods used by the ancient Egyptian mummy-makers. Instead, they cleaned and stuffed the body with good-smelling herbs and roots.

If the dead man were a chief, forty days before the burial he was carried around the lands he had ruled. His people followed his body, wailing and crying out their sorrow. Warriors on horseback rode along with the procession, stopping from time to time to put on a show about the riding and fighting skill of the dead chief. Members of the chief's family, and his servants, wore their finest clothing and walked along beside the body. The chief's best horses, with shining coats and harness, pulled carts carrying his personal belongings.

Probably about the same time, work on the tomb was started. It was dug into the ground and divided into a number of rooms with wood walls and ceilings. Each room would serve a special purpose.

Finally the burial time arrived. The chief's body uncovered, dressed in fine clothes, was placed inside the main room. Sometimes the body was placed in a huge wooden coffin made of a hollowed-out tree trunk. The chief's personal belongings, such as his weapons and his eating utensils, were placed near him, where he could reach them without difficulty when he awakened. The tomb's wooden walls were

THE BUBONIC PLAGUE SWEPT ACROSS EUROPE IN THE MIDDLE AGES. THIS EARLY WOODCUT SHOWS A MASS BURIAL WHERE MANY BODIES WERE PLACED SIDE BY SIDE IN LARGE GRAVES.

MANY ANCIENT PEOPLE BELIEVED THAT ONLY FIRE
COULD FREE THE SOUL OF A DEAD PERSON. BURNING,
OR CREMATING, IS THE SECOND OLDEST FORM OF DIS-
POSING OF A DEAD BODY.

ANCIENT EGYPTIANS THOUGHT MAN HAD BOTH A BODY
AND SPIRIT. UPON DEATH, THE SPIRIT WOULD BE SET
FREE. HERE THE SOUL, IN THE FORM OF A HUMAN-
HEADED BIRD, IS SHOWN HOVERING ABOVE A BODY PRE-
PARED FOR BURIAL.

IN ANCIENT EGYPT THE JACKAL WAS THOUGHT TO PLAY
A ROLE IN DEATH. IT WAS BELIEVED TO BE THE
GUARDIAN OF CEMETERIES AND WOULD LEAD THE DEAD
TO ITS PLACE OF JUDGMENT.

IN PARTS OF SICILY DURING THE MIDDLE AGES A SICK
PERSON WOULD LOOK FOR SUPERNATURAL SIGNS TO
TELL HIM IF HE WOULD GET WELL OR DIE. IT WAS BE-
LIEVED THAT IF A MYTHICAL BIRD LOOKED AT A PA-
TIENT HE WOULD LIVE; IF HE TURNED AWAY THE PER-
SON WOULD DIE.

draped with tapestries, and the chief's clothes were hung from hooks.

After the chief's burial chamber had been arranged, it was time to fill the other rooms. The chief's favorite wife, and sometimes other wives as well, were to join the chief in the afterlife, so they were killed and their bodies were then placed in wooden coffins in separate rooms. The Scythians were careful to give each woman the personal belongings she would need in the afterlife.

The chief's bodyguards, groom, cook, and other servants were killed too, and their bodies and tools were placed in the proper rooms. We don't know if any of the chief's wives or servants ever tried to run away. Very likely, though, they believed that in the afterlife they would go on much as before, so being killed might not have seemed so bad to them.

And, of course, the chief would need his horses in the afterlife, so his best ones were killed and buried just outside the wooden tomb walls.

When the tomb was as it should be, it was covered over with a mound of earth, the grave's only marker. Once the ceremony was over, the people and their new chief had finished their duty to their old leader, life on earth could go on.

The Lugbara, a tribe of east-central Africa, are an ancient people, who, in the last thirty years have come into contact with other people and other ways of believing and doing things. Like most of their ways, the old Lugbara way of dealing with death is changing. But about twenty-five years ago an anthropologist, a scientist who studies tribal ways, wrote about the Lugbara death customs and beliefs.

Like the Scythians, the Lugbara believed that life went on after death. The Scythians thought that the dead had no special ties to the world of the living. But the ties between the dead and the living was the only important thing about death for the Lugbara.

The Lugbara believed that the dead were important to the lives of their relatives. A dead person was as much respected as he had been when alive. When someone died, he was no longer a person "of the world outside." He became a person "in the earth." His body was no more and some part of him went to live somewhere beneath the ground.

The Lugbara did not care much about this world of the dead under the earth. They thought that probably the dead had some sort of ties with each other but this didn't matter to the living. What did matter were the ties between a dead person and his living family.

Each person on earth was thought to have a soul, called the "orindi." While a person was alive, his orindi was located in his heart. At death, the orindi went into the sky. The dead person became an ancestor. The Lugbara thought of all ancestors as good, wishing their family well. Ancestors were only important to their own family, not to others.

Still, most ancestors had no direct contact with their living relatives. Only a few important ancestors had a direct effect on their relatives' lives. In the case of the death of an important man in the tribe, a diviner, a special person in the tribe, contacted the dead man's orindi in the sky. Then the orindi returned to earth to live in a special shrine that the family had built. It was now known as the "ori," or ghost. The family made sacrifices to the ghost, and the ghost felt special responsibility toward his relatives.

When a Lugbara man died, the fire that burned in his compound was put out. The women in his family—his mother, aunts and wives—mourned for three days. They cried special mourning cries and covered themselves with ashes from the fire. For four days they would not wash or shave their heads, as they usually did.

When a woman died, the mourning usually lasted only three days. In this case too, the relatives would wail, wear ashes and not sweep their houses. Sometimes the husband of a dead woman would go off by himself to mourn.

The burial was taken care of by the relatives. When the family came together, a bull or a goat had to be given to certain of the relatives. Burial could not take place until the relatives had accepted the gift. If they did not accept, it meant that they believed the death was caused by witchcraft and the dead person might return to haunt them.

Most people were buried inside their own houses, in the center of the floor. The corpse was laid on a mat in a grave several feet deep. The right hand was placed beneath the head. Objects that showed the dead person's social position or job were placed in the grave. So a warrior might be buried with his weapons, while a wife was buried with her cooking utensils. Any possessions that were not buried were given to relatives.

The most important people in the tribe—tribal elders and old women who would have been elders if they had been men—were not buried indoors. The people feared that the elders' power was too great. It might harm those who lived in the house. So important people were buried outside, within the village.

Right after the burial, the death dances started. The living danced and sang songs about the dead person, telling how he or she lived and died. Depending on the importance of the person, the dances might continue for a day or two, or up to a week. The death dances for important people were big events. Many members of the tribe who weren't relatives came to them. Death dances might often be held several times over the following months for the tribe's elders.

The ordinary dead would usually fade from memory after the death dances. For the more important others, diviners contacted the orindi, the family settled any grievances the dead person might have against the living, and a shrine was built as a home for the ghost.

One group of people who lived very close to the Lugbara treated death in a very different way. The Pygmies of the central African forest wanted to forget death as soon as possible after it happened. Like the ancient Lugbara, the Pygmies are changing their old ways because they have met with the outside world. Today, Pygmy death customs might seem less strange to you than they would have only fifty or a hundred years ago.

The Pygmies used to name different degrees of sickness. If someone were feeling slightly ill, he was said to be "hot." Someone a little more ill was "ill." More serious degrees of illness were "dead," "completely dead," and finally, "dead for ever." When a person was "dead for ever," there was no hope of bringing him back.

The Pygmies did not believe in an afterlife. A person who was "dead for ever" was just gone. So it isn't surprising that the friends and relatives of a dead person were very unhappy. Men and women showed terrible grief.

Because death was such an unhappy event, the Pygmies felt it was better to return to normal life as soon as possible. The dead were usually buried the day they died. Then the Pygmies held a dance of death to make the forest happy again. The dance also helped to show their belief that the forest gives life but also takes it away. The Pygmies tried not to think about death because it was such an unhappy thing. Death didn't really frighten them, but they did feel a great loss when someone died.

In North America, thousands of miles away, another group of people did not like to think about death, but for a very different reason. The Navajo Indians of the American Southwest saw death as something awful and scary.

Navajos used to believe that life on this earth was the only thing that counted. They believed in a life after death, but there was no feeling that life would prepare the living for an afterlife. The Navajos thought that all the dead went to the same place, no matter if they had been good or bad.

The afterworld, where the dead lived, was thought to be under the earth's surface, somewhere toward the north, the direction of evil. It was reached by a long, downhill trail, with a pile of sand at the end. The living did not pretend to know exactly what this world of the dead was like, but they did not consider it good to think about it too much. They were very sure that it wasn't a happy place.

The Navajos believed strongly that they could be warned about death. If someone got one of the four warnings—noise in his windpipe, ringing in his ears, a twitching in his nose, a prickling on his skin—he took it as a sign that some awful thing, maybe death, was about to happen to him. The wise Navajo looked for help in doing the right ceremonies to side-step, or at least put off, the event.

The Navajos believed that when a person died, his dead relatives, who looked much as they had right before their own deaths, came to point out the path to the afterworld. The trip usually took four days. Upon getting there, the newly dead Navajo was given tests to make sure he was really dead.

Meanwhile, on earth, the relatives of the dead man would deal with the frightful matter as fast as possible. The dead person was taken out of the house through a hole cut in the north wall, because the door, which always faced east, was a holy direction. It would be bad if the body passed through it.

Burial of the body was done quickly, because it was considered a dangerous job. In fact, Navajos usually felt much better and very grateful if a stranger offered to take over.

Many personal belongings were buried with the body. Generally, before he died each person chose the things that would be buried with him. At the same time he usually named relatives who would get whatever he didn't want to take along. Any other belongings he forgot to give away himself were given away at a meeting of his relatives. Most of the time, the things that were used for important ceremonies were given to a man's sons or to his sisters' sons, who knew how to use them.

All those who took part in the burial were very careful to avoid touching the body. Afterward they had to be made pure again. Once their part was over they did not go near the grave. Only witches would go near a burial place! They even felt it might be unsafe to say the dead person's name.

Death was this frightening because they were afraid of ghosts. They saw a ghost as the evil part of a person. There was no such thing as a good ghost. Even if a person had been friendly and kind during life, his ghost was evil. Almost everyone became a ghost. Only people who died of old age and babies who did not live long enough to make a sound were harmless when they died.

The Navajos believed that living people could be evil too. For example, they believed in witches. But, wicked as they were, witches were human and so could be at least partly controlled. The evil of the dead was beyond the control of any living being.

Navajos thought that ghosts returned to earth because they had been hurt or insulted by the living. Most often, this involved some mistake in the funeral—the person was buried in an improper way, or he was not buried with some object he wanted, or he was not mourned long enough, or his grave had been disturbed.

Usually, ghosts came back to their graves or to their houses. They were more often seen at night, and for this reason, most Navajos were afraid to walk around in the dark. Ghosts could appear as human beings or as some night animal, such as an owl or a coyote. They could also be whirlwinds, spots of fire, or just dark shapes. Often they made noises, and they could change to any shape they wished.

Most of the time, a ghost didn't do any real damage right away. A person meeting a ghost was likely to be chased, hit, pulled at or have handfuls of dirt thrown at him. But the awful thing about meeting a ghost was the fact that it told about a misfortune to come; perhaps even one's own death. Even the most powerful ceremonies didn't always work.

Seeing death in this way, of course, the Navajos talked and thought about it as little as they could. They did not want to look at dead people or animals. They tried hard not to think about death at all. For them, the best way to deal with death was to pretend it did not exist.

CHAPTER THREE
DEATH AND RELIGION

SINCE EVERYONE WHO IS BORN WILL DIE, EACH group or society down through the ages has found a way of dealing with death. Every religion has held beliefs about what death is like, and ceremonies to go with those beliefs. In some religions, death ceremonies have become of great importance. In others, they play only a small role. But even for these religions, death must somehow be handled. No religion can meet the needs of its followers without giving them a way of seeing this difficult subject and a way of behaving when death happens.

Judaism, the Jewish religion, is one of the oldest in the world. It is thousands of years old. Yet, in all this time, Jewish writers and thinkers have developed few ideas about death and what it might be like. The Jewish religion deals more with life. Jews think, first of all, about how they should behave about God and with their fellow men. A religious Jew tries to lead a good life just because he believes that God wants him to. He does not spend much time thinking about being rewarded or punished after death.

The Jewish religion doesn't stop a Jew from believing in an afterlife. Jewish thinking doesn't say that death is a final end of life. Instead, Jews say that what happens after death isn't important. The present life is what matters.

Even so, Jews have a way of handling death in the community. Their ceremonies are simple ones, and show their feelings about death.

In many Jewish communities throughout the world, groups known as burial societies handle Jewish funerals and take care of Jewish cemeteries. A person who joins a burial society in his lifetime knows that when he dies, the proper things will be done and his family will not have to make decisions at a very sad time.

The Orthodox Jewish tradition forbids touching a person who is dying. This is not because a dying person is thought of as dangerous or unlucky, but because it might hasten his death.

Only when the family can be sure that death has come can they begin to prepare for the funeral. The windows in the house are opened wide. Mirrors are covered. Special prayers are said and members of the family will tear part of their clothing in certain ways. A family member, most likely an oldest son, closes the eyes and covers the face of the dead.

An hour after death, the dead person's body is placed on the floor, with the feet pointing toward the entrance of a room. A stone is placed under his head as a pillow and he is covered with a sheet. A lit candle is placed at his feet and another at his head.

The dead person should not be left alone. No one may bring food into the room, but a member of the family must stay in the room at all times. This is to make very sure that the person is truly dead.

Jewish law doesn't permit embalming or any other way of slowing down nature's process. The dead person is washed when the shroud or burial clothing has been made. The white shrouds must be made without hems or knots.

After all these things have been done, the dead person is ready for burial. In the Orthodox Jewish tradition, there is no coffin, but the laws of many countries today state that coffins must be used. Of course, Jews in these places follow the laws, just as they may follow other local laws and customs instead of their own traditions.

The Jews bury their dead, if possible, before the following day. In the old days, relatives and friends walked to the cemetery, carrying the dead on their shoulders. Today, in most countries, this is no longer done. There may be prayers said, and people tell about the dead person's life at home before the funeral, at the funeral home, or at the grave.

At the grave side, before burial, the dead person is addressed and asked to forgive any wrongs his family and friends may have done

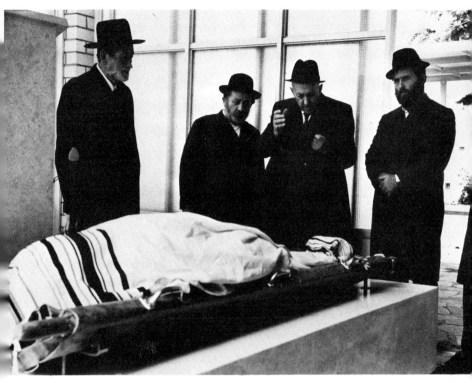

ORTHODOX JEWS ARE SHOWN CHANTING PRAYERS
AROUND A BODY BEFORE BURIAL. THE BODY IS COVERED
WITH A PRAYER SHAWL.

him, and to depart in peace. As they leave the cemetery, some of the mourners may pick a few blades of grass and toss them over their shoulders, saying, "He remembereth that we are as dust."

Orthodox Jews also have rules for mourning. The mourning begins right after burial. Members of the family are not allowed to cook their first meal, the Meal of Condolence. Food is brought in by neighbors. For the first three days of mourning, no one can work. During the next four days, work is allowed, but a number of things must be done. For the whole first week, there are two daily prayer services at the mourners' house.

Following the first week, there is a twenty-day period of mourning, with fewer prayers said. On the anniversary of the death of a parent, children are expected to fast, to go to services at a synagogue, and to recite a special prayer for the dead at home.

The Christian religion, which grew out of Judaism, has somewhat different ideas about death. Death is a far more important event for Christians. It seems that early Christians felt a need to know more of what death was like.

And so they spent much time thinking about what could happen to them after their life on earth stopped.

Christians were sure that some part of a human being, the soul, lived on after the person died. Like Jews, Christians have always felt that a person's thoughts and deeds in his life on earth are important. But while Jews feel that they are important in themselves, Christians believe that deeds are important because they influence what will become of a person's soul when his body dies.

Christians believe that people who lead good lives on earth will get their rewards after death; that evil people will be punished when they die. Many Christians think that good souls go to heaven where they will live forever with God, while evil souls go to hell where Satan rules. Ideas of what heaven and hell are like, and how a person can get to heaven and stay out of hell, differ among Catholics and the many Protestant groups. Some Christians do not even believe in hell at all. But all Christians believe in the life of the soul after the death of the body, and most believe in the idea of rewards and punishments.

Since few Christian groups have rules that must be followed about funerals, and since there are Christian communities all over the world, Christian funeral customs change from country to country. Most Protestant groups follow local law, custom, and the wishes of the family.

Roman Catholics do have a few rules to keep. When someone is dying, a priest should be called as quickly as possible. The priest is important because it is best that the dying person be forgiven for his sins before he can enter into heaven. Catholic funerals should be held in church. While there are certain ways or rules for the use of flowers, and placing the coffin, candles, and other things inside the church, most of the details are up to the family.

In the United States, most Protestant funerals are much alike except for small differences preferred by separate groups, or sects, the region of the country, and the wishes of the family. The dead person is taken to a funeral home right away. Here, embalming, a way of preserving the body, is taken care of. For one or more days people visit the funeral home. They come to pay their respects to the family and sometimes to see, for the last time, their friend or relative who has died and who seems to be just sleeping peacefully in his coffin. The funeral service may be held in church or in the funeral home. Usually prayers are said, there is a reading from the Bible, a special sermon by a minister, and music. At the cemetery there is often another short service before burial.

Most of the dead, in the United States, rest in cemeteries, in coffins buried in the ground. Some coffins are placed in above-ground mausoleums, small stone buildings on the cemetery grounds.

A growing number of people in the United States prefer the idea of cremation, much used in the East and in Protestant countries of Europe. These people don't like the idea of the body remaining when life, or the soul, has left. They feel that cremating, or burning to ashes, is better.

Mohammedism is the third great religion —born in the Middle East. The prophet Mohammed founded the nation of Islam and the Mohammed or Islamic faith. He studied and was affected by the Bible and other Christian and Jewish writings. Islamic beliefs about what

NATIVES OF NEW GUINEA ARE SHOWN CARRYING A DEAD
TRIBESMAN FOR BURIAL. THE BODY IS WRAPPED AND
CARRIED BY WOMEN ON A STRETCHER WITH POLES OF
LIGHT BAMBOO.

A JAPANESE WOMAN IS SHOWN LOOKING AT A HIGHLY
DECORATED HEARSE. A CASKET IS USUALLY PLACED IN-
SIDE THE HEARSE AND PULLED TO ITS BURIAL PLACE.

}49}

happens after death are close to Christian ones. Moslems, people who follow the teachings of Mohammed, believe that the good are rewarded and the wicked punished after death. Good people, who have obeyed the Koran, Islam's holy book, go to paradise when they die. The wicked, who have broken Allah's, the God of Islam, laws will live in a hell forever.

As with Christians and Jews, Moslem funeral customs change from one place to another. In most Arab countries in the Middle East today, a Moslem funeral consists of a number of rules with local customs added, and is usually simple and quick.

Moslems do not have priests as a separate class. So the family is supposed to take care of all the details of the funeral. Often, though, a local holy man or tribal leader will prepare the dead for burial. This is very often done in country areas. Once the dead body has been washed and wrapped in linen, it is placed in a simple wooden coffin made by carpenters not related to the family. After the coffin is made the family and friends take over.

For Moslems, going to a funeral is a good deed that finds favor with Allah. Even better than just going is the chance to carry the coffin. Often, so many friends and relatives want to help carry the coffin that they have to take turns to give everyone a chance. The funeral party walks slowly toward the place where the service will be held. Everyone walks, including those carrying the coffin. Mohammed taught that angels walk along in front of the body. If angels walk, it would not be right for men to ride.

When an important person in the community dies, the funeral service is almost always held in a mosque, or Moslem temple. An ordinary person's funeral service may also take place in a mosque or in an open space near the person's home. The service is never held in a cemetery because they are thought of as unclean.

The nearest living relative of the person who has died is supposed to recite the special service for the dead. And he may add some remarks of his own. When all the prayers and readings are over, the mourners sit for a while in silence. Finally, friends and neighbors tell the family that the death was the will of God. The nearest relative answers, "I am pleased with the will of God." This ends the funeral service.

Few people attend the burial, but great care must be taken with the body after the service, since Moslems believe that the dead can feel pain. For this reason, too, the dead are buried in the earth, not cremated. At the grave, the body is taken from the coffin and gently placed in the earth, facing Mecca, the Moslem holy city.

The religions of the Eastern world see death in ways that may seem strange to Westerners. And Western ideas are difficult for many Asians to understand. Many people in the West see death as an ending. Others think about it as the beginning of a new kind of life—an afterlife. But to followers of Eastern religions death isn't a beginning or an ending. A life and death is seen as just one small part or segment of a great circle.

Hinduism is the major religion of India, and so the way that millions of people think. Hindus believe that who and what they are in their present lives on earth has been decided by their behavior when they lived before in another time on earth.

Each living thing, according to Hindu thought, goes through many, many lives, deaths,

MOSLEMS BELIEVE THAT A DEAD BODY STILL FEELS PAIN. THE CASKET MUST BE VERY CAREFULLY CARRIED TO ITS BURIAL PLACE IN THE EARTH. MOSLEMS CONSIDER IT A GREAT HONOR TO HELP CARRY THE CASKET.

and rebirths. A Hindu hopes that after many lives he will leave the great circle and not be reborn. Instead, he will become one with Brahma, or, in other words, a part of the universe. This is a little difficult for us to understand because we like to think of being ourselves even after death. For Hindus, however, the idea of not being a special person and becoming one tiny part of the great force of the universe is very wonderful.

Hinduism sees death as a natural part of the circle, freeing a soul so that it may go again on the path toward a final goal. But the dying person may feel sad to leave the happiness he has found in his present life. And his family will feel sad because they will miss him.

Although death is a natural part of the circle, there are special ceremonies when death comes. These ceremonies help make the soul pure and be reborn. In the first place, it is a good idea for a dying person to be free of sins. Many times, people close to death will travel to a holy city to wash themselves clean of sins in sacred waters. If they are unable to make the journey, they may confess their sins to a priest. Or a friend can take on the burden of these sins so that the dying can be pure. Later, the friend can travel to the holy city and wash away the sins he has taken on.

When someone dies, relatives have a number of duties. The body must be arranged. It is draped with flowers and a lamp is placed near the head.

While this is going on, other relatives mourn loudly. Friends and neighbors come to pay their respects to the family and to see the flower-draped body, since few people will come to the funeral.

After the visitors have left, the family must get ready for the funeral. The dead person's head is touched with oil by the chief heir, and again by other close relatives. Then, wrapped in white linen, dressed in funeral clothing, and decorated with white clay, the dead person is placed on a stretcher to be carried by close relatives to the funeral place. Here there is a short ceremony. The body is smeared with "ghee," a sacred butter, and placed on a funeral pyre. The chief mourner, a close relative, lights the pyre while members of the family march around it.

On the third day after cremation, the fam-

HINDUS, UNLIKE MOSLEMS, BELIEVE THAT A BODY MUST BE CREMATED. THE BODY CANNOT BE PLACED IN A CASKET BUT WRAPPED IN A WHITE CLOTH (LEFT) AND BROUGHT ON A STRETCHER TO THE FUNERAL PYRE (ABOVE) WHERE IT WILL BE BURNED. THE CLOSEST RELATIVE WILL LIGHT THE FIRE.

ily meets once more at the funeral place. A priest reads from the sacred books, sprinkles holy water, and collects whatever bones have not been consumed by the fire. These he places in a vase which he gives to a relative. Poor people generally toss these into the nearest body of water because Hindus believe that all waters flow into the sacred Ganges River. Wealthier families, who can afford to travel to the Ganges at a later date, bury the vase until they can go to the river.

Immediately after the cremation, the family must begin a ten-day ceremony to make sure that the soul of the dead person gets a new body. Without these ceremonies it is feared that the soul may be given only part of a body, or none at all. Through the family's neglect, it may roam space as an evil spirit. During this time, other people stay away because the family of the dead person is considered unclean.

On the tenth day, the soul's body is complete. But before it can travel to the place where it will be born again, it must be given the right food. To do this the family must have what is called the "sraddha" between the tenth and thirty-first day. The person who will oversee the ceremony of sraddha goes barefooted to the houses of his relatives to invite them. Everyone brings food and gifts for the soul of the dead person. Following this, the vase is dug up and the bones are cast into the Ganges. This is the final ceremony. Now the soul can be reborn.

Buddhism is another great religion of the East. Although it started in India, it has spread to other countries of Asia. While certain Buddhist beliefs are the same everywhere, each country has changed them a little to fit in with its own way of life.

In Tibet, a lonely land in the Himalayas, a new form of Buddhism appeared. Dealing with the problem of death became one of the most important parts of the Tibetan religion.

Tibetans think birth is not a very happy event. While the birth of a child certainly isn't a reason to be unhappy, it isn't a reason for celebrating. And death isn't a good reason to have a party, but on the other hand, it isn't a very sad time. Like Hindus, Buddhists believe that death is not final, but only one link in a chain of many lives.

Each person dies and is reborn over and

over again. Each person hopes that he will be reborn to live a religious life. Finally, he may reach nirvana and break out of the circle of death and rebirth, *if he doesn't hope for it to happen*. Nirvana means a losing of the self so as to become one with all things. It can't be hoped for because it comes only to those who do not wish for it.

So most Buddhists of Tibet expect to be reborn when they die. There is, however, a journey that the soul of the newly dead must take first. For forty-nine days the soul travels through "bardo," between death and rebirth. The journey "between the two" is full of danger. One wrong step and the soul might wind up in one of the Buddhist hells forever instead of returning to earth.

To make sure that each person's soul can pass safely through bardo, the Tibetan Buddhists have many ceremonies to be performed by the dead soul, his living relatives, and lamas —Buddhist priests. When a Tibetan is dying, his family must call a lama, or if possible, several lamas—as many as they can afford to pay. One lama must watch the dying person so that the "passing ceremony" can be performed at the moment of death. Everyone must leave the room while the lama pulls a single hair from the head of the person who has just died. Using secret, mystical words, the lama calls upon the soul to leave the body through the tiny hole that held the hair. Even though the soul leaves the body in this way, it stays nearby. No soul knows the right path through bardo, but must be taught by a lama reading the *Bardo-Todol*, the Tibetan Book of the Dead.

The living relatives need to be informed too, for their help is needed to guide the soul along the right path. An astrologer, a person who can read messages in the stars, is brought in. He finds out from the stars who may touch the body, what prayers should be said, and other important matters.

Only when these things have been decided can news of the death be sent out. Relatives and friends begin to arrive at the house, bringing money and gifts to help pay the lamas for their services. For three days the lamas stay with the dead and chant to send the soul on its way. The family continues to bring food for the dead person during this time as if the person still lived. After three days a feast is held. The family prepares a great meal for the dead. A lama presents the food to the corpse along with a long silk scarf, saying, "You have now received from your relatives all this good food and drink. Take freely of it, as you shall not have another chance of doing so. For you must understand that you have died and your spirit must go from here, and never again come back to trouble or hurt your relatives. Come this way."

A funeral band of three men is formed. First comes a lama, blowing a trumpet and ringing a bell. Then comes the lama holding one end of the scarf, the other end tied to the body held by the "ragyapa," he who carries the dead.

The three go alone to the burial place. Meanwhile, friends, relatives, and other lamas must drive the death-causing demon from the house. A demon figure is made, a large unpleasant-looking doll. At nightfall the ceremony begins with the chanting of a lama. Men pick up their weapons and fight the demon. When the lama decides that the demon has been killed he carries the demon doll out of the house. To stop the demon from going into neighboring homes, he draws magical circles around the houses.

But the family still has more to do. For forty-nine days they must perform the proper ceremonies. Each day they must offer food to a picture of their relative now supposed to be traveling through bardo. Then they must burn the picture. An astrologer tells about the soul's progress from the shape taken by the smoke and the color of the flame.

Every seventh day during bardo, the family must offer special prayers and pay the lamas who are helping them. After forty-nine days, the ceremonies are over and the soul is ready to be reborn.

CHAPTER FOUR
THE WAR AGAINST DEATH

IF YOU HAD BEEN BORN IN ANCIENT TIMES, YOU would have been elderly before the age of thirty. If you had been born in the 1700s, you could have expected to live to the great old age of forty. If you were born in the 1960s, you are likely to enjoy birthday parties with more than seventy candles on the cake. And this is true because of the many advances in medicine.

The history of medicine is the story of a fight against death. Since there have been doctors, they have done whatever they could to save life. In the beginning, what they could do wasn't very much. Today, what they can do is a great deal. And every day new weapons or new ways to fight death are found so that we have a better and better chance of living longer and longer.

Most likely, even the earliest people tried to cure the sick and prevent death. The first men found good-tasting plants growing wild in the fields and woods. They may also have discovered that some of these plants stopped pain or helped sick people get well.

These early men thought of illness as a punishment, perhaps sent by some angry god. Or they believed that an evil spirit coming to live inside the body was the cause of pain or sickness. So the doctor's job was to make peace with the angry god, or to make the evil spirit go away.

Men who knew how to make medicines, who learned the right things to say to gods and spirits, who could cheat death, were important and powerful people. "Doctoring" became a special job and a profession that brought many honors. Sometimes the early doctors really did find cures: herbs, plants and roots that really helped. In fact, some of the medicines of today are closely related to ancient cures. But with these first doctors, a success was often just lucky chance. Often they could do no good at all, and sometimes, without meaning to, they did a lot more harm than good.

We know that the practice of medicine was an important skill in past civilizations. In Babylonia, there were special laws about the work of doctors. Five-thousand-year-old medical books used in Egypt have been found. And ancient Indian doctors knew a great deal about curative drugs made from plants, and were in some cases able to perform operations.

But it was in ancient Greece that the practice of medicine really changed from a magic to a science. Hippocrates, born in Greece in 460 B.C., was a doctor and a teacher. His ideas were so important that he is known as the father of medicine.

Hippocrates disagreed with other men of his time that sickness was caused by the gods. Over and over again in his writings, he said that every illness has a natural cause, even if that cause can't be seen. He said also that a person's way of life—the food eaten, the work done, and the climate lived in—was important, causing either sickness or health. The promise he made, called the Hippocractic oath, is with few changes, the model for the behavior of medical men today.

For many centuries after Hippocrates the science of medicine changed very little. In many parts of the world, people had never heard of Hippocrates. Even where his name and teachings were known, they were often not accepted. Many people kept right on believing that illness was the punishment of the gods. And doctors who wanted to learn about the natural causes of sickness were in danger of breaking the laws and of the disapproval of others. For example, they were unable to use the dead to learn anatomy, the study of the human body and its parts. Not much happened in medicine in the Western world until around the year 1300.

At that time, in Europe, people began to question old ways of doing things. They began to listen and think about new ideas and put aside old beliefs. In medicine, this new spirit led to the careful observation of disease and to a scientific study of human anatomy. Better methods in surgery were found too, because doctors and surgeons performed operations and learned from these experiences. Medical schools opened and taught the new ways.

In the next few hundred years this open-minded thinking led to a number of advances and to the beginnings of modern medicine. In the early part of the seventeenth century, William Harvey discovered the way blood circulates through the body. Before Harvey discovered that arteries carry the blood from the heart and veins return it, doctors believed that blood ebbed and flowed in the blood vessels in some way, like ocean tides. Even more important than the discovery of the circulatory system, was the scientific method Harvey had used.

At the same time, doctors and other scientists were working on new medical tools. Among the most important was the microscope. With this invention, doctors could see much smaller things than they had been able to see before, using only their eyes.

During the eighteenth century, doctors began to learn the importance of stopping sickness and disease before it started. The field of preventive medicine came into being. Medicine had come a long way from the time when a doctor's job was to drive away spirits and demons. But in one way it had traveled backward. It had returned to the teachings of Hippocrates who was the first to say that medicine should prevent disease by ending unhealthy living conditions.

One of the eighteenth century's most exciting discoveries in preventive medicine was vaccination. Vaccination gives a person a very light case of a disease that does not harm him so that he will not catch the disease a second time. Edward Jenner, an English country doctor, is usually given the credit for developing the vaccination for smallpox. In this case, Jenner gave his patients a light case of a disease called "cowpox," and found that this prevented smallpox. In Jenner's day, smallpox was common and easy to catch. Many people died during smallpox epidemics.

By the beginning of the nineteenth century, doctors had learned where and what most of the body organs were, and what part each played in the life process. But there were still many important discoveries to come. Probably this century's most important find was that many diseases are caused by tiny, living things.

For hundreds of years, the idea existed that disease might be caused by particles, like flecks of dust, too small to be seen going into the body. But it was Louis Pasteur, a French chemist, who proved by experiment that disease could be caused by tiny *living* things called *bacteria*.

Surgical advances were made at this time, as well. Joseph Lister used Pasteur's findings to prove the importance of *antiseptic* surgery. The word "antiseptic" means against infection—or in plain language—clean. Before Pasteur and Lister, doctors never worried about how clean they ought to be. Many people died, not from operations alone, but because bacteria in the operating room, on surgical tools, and on doctor's hands caused infection.

General anesthetics were developed, gases and drugs that could be safely used by doctors to put patients to sleep and kill pain. Because of anesthetics, doctors were able to perform longer, more difficult operations than before.

By the beginning of the twentieth century, medicine was truly a science. Doctors had

(TOP LEFT) LOUIS PASTEUR (1822–95) WAS ONE OF THE GIANTS OF MEDICAL DISCOVERY. HIS WORK WITH HUMANS AND OTHER ANIMALS GAVE MAN NEW KNOWLEDGE ABOUT SUCH DREAD DISEASES AS RABIES, ANTHRAX, AND CHOLERA.

(TOP RIGHT) JOSEPH LISTER (1827–1912) SAW MANY OF HIS PATIENTS DIE FROM INFECTION AFTER SURGERY. HE BELIEVED THAT INFECTION WAS CAUSED BY BACTERIA ENTERING THE PATIENT'S BODY DURING AN OPERATION. HE BEGAN TO SPRAY AN ANTISEPTIC AROUND THE SURGICAL WOUND AND DISCOVERED THAT INFECTIONS HAD BEEN STOPPED.

learned ways of curing that would have seemed like miracles to doctors of the seventeenth century. But in one important way, they had not come very far. They had not added many years to people's lives. In 1900, a person could only expect to live fifty years or less.

The first seventy years of the twentieth century saw more medical advances than in all the past years of human history—advances that lengthened life. Doctors found that certain chemicals were able to fight certain diseases. Penicillin, discovered accidentally by Alexander Fleming in 1928 helped to fight a great number of diseases caused by bacteria. Used during World War II, it saved thousands of lives.

Penicillin was a great lifesaver, but it was not a cure for all bacterial diseases. It did not, for example, kill the bacteria that causes tuberculosis. But, with the idea of using special drugs (antibiotics) for special diseases, scientists searched and were able to find drugs to fight tuberculosis. A number of other antibiotics were developed during the 1950s and 1960s. And twentieth-century doctors and researchers kept on looking for better ways to prevent, as well as cure, disease. This meant more work on vaccinations. Early in the century, vaccines were developed that prevented typhoid fever, tetanus, and diptheria. In those countries like the United States, where children were given the new vaccines as part of their general health care, these feared diseases almost disappeared.

Vaccinations for virus diseases were harder to develop. Viruses are much, much smaller than bacteria, and so are harder to find and separate. Even though we know now that smallpox is a virus disease, when Edward Jenner made his smallpox vaccine, viruses were unknown. And except for smallpox, virus diseases could not be prevented until nearly the middle of the twentieth century.

After researchers found ways of growing viruses in laboratories and the powerful microscopes to study them, real progress could be made. Soon, a vaccine for yellow fever was developed. Later, came vaccines against influenza (the flu) and poliomyelitis (polio). During the 1960s, doctors developed vaccinations against measles and German measles.

How many vaccinations have you had during your life? When you were a baby you were probably given the vaccines for typhoid, tetanus, diptheria, and smallpox, and you probably had a vaccine test to find out if you had been around anyone who had tuberculosis. Later on you had the vaccines for polio and measles, and perhaps one to keep you from catching the flu during an epidemic.

So many new discoveries have been made in this century they can't all be written about outside of a medical textbook. A whole new branch of medicine called "endocrinoly" has developed because so much has been learned about the importance of the endocrine glands. These glands produce different hormones, chemical substances needed in the body. Insulin is a hormone needed to turn food starches and sugars into energy. Some people are unable to produce enough insulin in their bodies. This used to be the cause of a serious disease called diabetes. But today, insulin is manufactured, diabetics take it and can lead normal, active lives.

Another discovery that is saving lives and preventing disease today, is that vitamins exist in food and are important to good health. Before scientists found out about vitamins, people who ate too much of one kind of food and not enough of others, suffered from diseases caused by vitamin deficiencies. Most people today try to stay on a balanced diet and eat the kinds of foods that give them all the vitamins they need.

And surgery has made a giant leap forward helped by inventions in other fields of knowledge as well as medical science. New machines and new materials such as plastic and lightweight metals have been important to medicine. Broken bones can be patched up to be stronger than before. And other parts, organs of the body that need correcting or just wear out can be patched, or in some cases, replaced. This is almost like a new gas pump, or muffler, or fanbelt can be replaced in a car to make it run again. At the beginning of the 1900s, there were many operations that doctors wouldn't even try. Then, discoveries of new drugs made doctors feel that most infections could be prevented or cured. Free of the worry of causing disease during operation, surgery continues to advance.

Some science-fiction stories tell about people in a frozen sleep waking up a thousand years into the future. This idea isn't so far away from medical possibility. Doctors now use very low temperatures as a tool of surgery, and experiments in this area are going on. The idea of operating in hospitals built on satellites in outer space is a possibility of the not-too-far-off future. The fact that the body is weightless in outer space might help in surgery cases.

Some people believe that soon man may win his fight over death—that it could be in your lifetime. Doctors may learn how to stop people from growing old so that no one dies of old age.

In this new world, some few people might still die in accidents. For most people, though, death could become something they read about in history books, not meet in their own daily lives. For the first time in history, life and death would not go hand in hand. There would be life without death.

What would it be like to live in a world where death was unusual? Any death that happened would interest everyone. Maybe a story like the following one would be on the front page of your local newspaper.

MAN DIES HERE TODAY

Last night, James Nelson went for a walk. When his wife, Martha, woke up this morning, her husband had not come back. Concerned, she called the police.

On the way to the Nelson house to take the missing persons report, Sergeant Thomas Young saw a man lying in the road. He stopped, lifted the man into his car, and rushed him to the nearest hospital. The man proved to be James Nelson.

After doctors had examined and consulted, they reported that Nelson was dead. Asked why it had taken four hours to decide that the patient must be dead, a spokesman for the hospital stated, "Doctors here have read about death, of course. But none had handled a patient in this condition. We had to be certain that the man was dead."

The doctors believe that Nelson was struck by a car. If he had been taken to a hospital right after the accident, he could easily have been saved. As any driver would know this and would be expected to stop and help, foul play is suspected. Police are investigating.

James Nelson would have been 104 years old in October. Nelson's family physician, reached by videophone said, "What a tragedy. Such a young man! Just last year, I removed his old, worn out stomach and replaced it with a plastic one. Why, he was always such a healthy fellow, except for a slight case of lung cancer cured seventeen years ago. I can't believe it. He was in the prime of condition."

Today, the Nelson family must decide what to do with the body. The city health commissioner has been asked for a special burial permit in one of the old cemeteries. This is the first death in the city in more than fifty years.

Try to imagine your own life in a world where no one ever dies. In such a world you would have a chance to meet people you have read about in history books. You might discover that you had some interesting ancestors. You would have many to choose from: two parents, four grandparents, eight great-grandparents, sixteen great-great-grandparents, thirty-two great-great-great-grandparents, and so on. If you kept counting backward, you would have to keep doubling the number of your ancestors.

This imaginary world might be interesting, at least for a while, but it probably would also be very crowded. Most of the earth's space would be taken up by places for all the people to live. Many, many people would have to live in each house. Even if only relatives had to live together, you might find yourself sharing your room with 1,024 great-great-great-great-great-great-great-great-grandmothers.

If you could stand the crowding, you might grow up and have children of your own. They would have to live in the same house too, along with the children of your brothers and sisters and of your thousands and thousands of cousins.

Finally, there would be no room on earth for more people. Governments probably would not permit any more babies to be born. People already living would just get older and older and older.

The idea of such a world may seem very appealing. As sad as people may feel at the death of a friend, or how they may feel at the thought of their own death, they aren't all sure how good it would be to win the war against death. A world without death, and so, after a while, without new life, seems unnatural.

Many people who have thought about this, feel that conquering death is not to be desired. Yet, the age-old promise of medicine is to preserve life as long as possible, to use every means at hand to prevent death. Every day, doctors learn ways to extend life. Should doctors continue to use all they know to preserve life? Should they continue to search for new life-saving methods or should each person be permitted to decide whether or not his life should be preserved?

Tony Gallo was not an old man—he was in his fifties—when doctors told him he had a disease that could not be cured. Gallo might have been saved by a transplant to give him a new kidney, but his high blood pressure made the operation too dangerous. Instead, he had to start using a kidney machine. The machine did the work his kidneys couldn't do.

Surely this treatment was a miracle. But it was a high-priced miracle. Tony Gallo was not a rich man. The treatments three times a week, six hours each time, used up his family's savings and put them into debt. He never felt really well. He was permitted to eat and drink very little, and he was not allowed meat. If he ate or drank more than he was supposed to, it made him feel dizzy or weak.

Finally, Tony Gallo had had enough. Two years after beginning treatments he decided to stop taking them. He felt his life was no longer worth living.

Gallo's decision upset his friends and relatives. They begged him to continue the treatments but he would not do so. One week later Tony Gallo died.

This man probably could have lived for

many years not feeling too well, or comfortable. Was he wrong to end his own life? Suppose he had been well, but very unhappy. Is it wrong for a person with a healthy body to take his own life? If someone in bodily pain is allowed to die, should the same right be given to someone who is feeling the pain of sadness and unhappiness? And what about someone who is suffering but unable to decide about his own life or death? Should others be able to decide for him and help such a person die?

Phyllis and Paul Obernauer had three healthy, normal children. Their fourth child was different. The fourth baby was born too early and was mentally retarded. Other physical problems led doctors to say that without an operation the baby would die.

Phyllis Obernauer talked to the doctors to find out what kind of life the baby would have. She found that the baby would grow up weak and sickly, and would need more surgery. Because she was retarded she would never be able to care for herself. She would always have to be cared for by others in the family.

The child's mother decided not to permit

the operation. It would be kinder for everyone, she thought, to let the baby die.

Most people were shocked and angry. Through law, the doctors forced the operation. Even afterward, the baby almost died. Finally, after months of costly treatment that the Obernauers could not really afford, the baby was able to leave the hospital.

Phyllis Obernauer agreed to take care of the baby. Yet, just as she had thought, life became very difficult for the rest of the family. Had she been right to feel the baby should have been allowed to die at birth?

Questions like these, in an already crowded world, grow more important as doctors gain new knowledge and new skills to preserve life. People may have to change their strongest feelings about life and death. Already, many people are beginning to say that the kind of life being lived is more important than the fact of life itself.

It seems unlikely that all people will find the same answers for these questions of life and death. We will continue to disagree until, or unless, death's mystery can be solved. And then, of course, there will be other questions.

INDEX

Anatomy, human, scientific study of, 67–68
Ancestors, 30, 78
Ancient people, death beliefs of, 15–38
  Japanese shell-heap builders, 17–20
  Lugbara tribe, 29–33
  Navajo Indians, 34–38
  Pygmies, 33–34
  Scythians, 20–29
Anesthetics, development of, 70
Anniversary prayer, 44
Anthrax, 71
Anthropologists, 29
Antibiotics, 72
Antiseptic surgery, importance of, 70, 71
Astrologers, 61

Babylonia (ancient), 66
Bacterial diseases, 72
Bardo, journey through, 60, 63
Bardo-Todol (Tibetan Book of the Dead), 61
Barnard, Dr. Christiaan, 8–11
Bible, 47
Brahma, 54
Bubonic Plague, 23
Buddhism, 59
Burial societies, Jewish, 40–41

Cavemen, 17
Cholera, 71
Christianity, 44–47, 50
  afterlife beliefs, 44–45
  funeral customs, 46–47
Circulatory system, discovery of, 68
Clothing, tearing of, 41
Cowpox, 69
Cremation
  in ancient times, 24
  Hindu, 55–58, 59
  in the United States, 47

Death
  ancient beliefs about, 15–38
  birth and, 1, 16
  fear of, 3, 13
  heart beat and, 5–7
  as an irreversible coma, 12–13
  living in a world without, 76–79
  meaning of, 1–13
  and religion, 39–63
  school courses about, 4
  and taking your own life, 80–82
  war against, 64–82
Death dances, 32
Diabetes, 74
Diphtheria, 73, 74
Diseases, causes of, 70
Doctors, beginning of, 65–67
Donors, heart transplant, 9–10
Dying person
  last thoughts of, 4–5
  priest and, 46

Egypt (ancient), 25, 66
  body and spirit beliefs, 25

INDEX

A native of New York, Stanley Klein, author of *The Final Mystery*, was graduated from New York University with a degree in both chemistry and history. He has taught both elementary and junior high school students and was also a professor at Southern Connecticut State College. It was there that he discovered his love for writing for children, and he spent about five years as a writer-editor of a nationally circulated elementary school classroom newspaper. He is now teaching at Western Connecticut State College and is the president of an educational consulting firm. Mr. Klein lives in Stamford, Connecticut, with his wife and daughters.